Trevor Wye
PRACTICE BOOK
for the Flute

Book 1
Tone

T0078991

Contents

Novello

For Micky

Published by
Novello Publishing Limited
14-15 Berners Street,
London W1T 3LJ, UK.

Exclusive Distributors:
Music Sales Limited
Distribution Centre, Newmarket Road,
Bury St Edmunds, Suffolk IP33 3YB, UK.

Music Sales Corporation
180 Madison Avenue, 24th Floor,
New York NY 10016, USA.

Music Sales Pty Limited
Units 3-4, 17 Willfox Street, Condell Park
NSW 2200, Australia.

Edited by Toby Knowles.
Music designed by Paul Ewers Music Design.

Printed in the EU.

www.musicsales.com

The Practice Book series is about effective practice: how to extract the most from it, how to be more skilled at it and how to isolate and overcome the problems and difficulties encountered in performing. It was written to help you achieve good results in the shortest time. If the advice is followed and the exercises practised properly, they will shorten the time taken to achieve success in the basics of flute playing and allow more time for music making.

Practising

Practise because you want to. If you don't want to – don't. It is almost useless spending your practice time practising, but wishing that you weren't. Having decided to practise seriously, make it difficult. Examine all aspects of your tone, intonation and technique for flaws and practise to remove them. You will then make rapid progress. Practise what you can't play, or practise a technique you are not familiar with. Try not to indulge in too much self-flattery by playing through pieces or exercises you can already play well.

Many of these exercises are strenuous so be sure your posture and hand positions are correct. Consult a good teacher or if you are in doubt, refer to *Practice Book 6 – Advanced Practice* (Novello) or look at *Efficient Practice* (Trevor Wye; Falls House Press), or *Proper Flute Playing* (Novello), which contains a practice guide on how best to schedule these exercises.

How to make the best use of your practice time

Most of us have a limit on how much time we have to practise. Let's assume that the four subjects below are the priority. Each should take up about one quarter of your total technical practice time, though this can be varied according to needs:

Tone • Expression and Intonation • Technique • Scales and Arpeggios

Articulation needs extra time, although if your articulation is good, you can incorporate this into scales and technique sessions by varying the articulation patterns as shown in the *Technique* and *Breathing & Scales* Practice Books. *Practice Book 3 – Articulation* suggests ways to achieve clear and rapid tonguing effectively. Of course you will have other subjects to work on too, but this is a practical scheme which will help most people. Technique (finger independence) is not quite the same as scales and arpeggios, which are the building blocks of musical composition. Scales and arpeggios are set out in *Practice Book 5*. Technique and finger independence exercises can be found in *Practice Book 2* and also in *Practice Book 6 – Advanced Practice*.

GUARANTEE

Possession of this book is no guarantee that you will improve on the flute; there is no magic in the printed paper. But, if you have the desire to play well and if you put in some diligent practice, you cannot fail to improve. It is simply a question of *time, patience* and *intelligent* work. The book is designed to avoid unnecessary practice. It is concentrated stuff. Provided that you follow the instructions carefully, you should make more than twice the improvement in half the time!

That is the guarantee.

This is one of a series of six basic exercise books for players of all ages who have been learning the flute from about a year upwards and including those at college or university. The exercises are spread out over the six books and should be selected and practised as needed. The speeds of the exercises should be chosen to accommodate the skill and age of the player. Some exercises are more difficult than others. Simply use those that are the most useful.

The other books in this series are:

PRACTICE BOOK for the Flute

These books were revised and updated in 2013.
© Trevor Wye

A Plan For Using This Book

TONE EXERCISES

General Observations

This book is not concerned with any particular school of flute playing, national style or concept of sound production. It is a simply a guide to making a beautiful tone throughout the compass of the flute. Play the exercises with your eyes closed as it will enhance your perception and your hearing. A good teacher will be of help.

Listen carefully while you are playing and try not to be distracted by events or noises around you. Tone exercises are better started in the low register and built upwards as the second octave is already contained in the low notes as the second harmonic and you should build on that.

We should bear in mind the preface to Marcel Moyse admirable book, *De la Sonorité*, in which he writes, 'It is all a question of *time, patience and intelligent work*.'

Possession of this book is not enough to ensure success.

TONE

The word 'tone' is a collective noun for a formula containing a number of ingredients, each of which contributes significantly to the concept of tone, for example: colour, size, projection, intensity, vibrato, loudness and purity. If your tone contains these ingredients, it might be regarded as beautiful but your tone is only as good as its weakest part. It isn't possible to practise any one of these qualities without incorporating the others. Anyone who desires to make a beautiful tone will get, at the very least, a tone which gives some pleasure and enjoyment. Long slow tones by themselves give the player the opportunity to examine their tone in fine detail and allows time to hear undesirable aspects of it and to make corrections accordingly. Long tones really can't fail to help improve your tone, though if played without care or thought won't achieve a result so quickly. That will only come with *time, patience* and *intelligent work,* using the series of steps in this book.

HARMONICS

Harmonics are the ingredients which make up sound or tone. When they are mixed in with the basic tone, (the fundamental, or first harmonic), they give tone its colour and character.

For younger players, the low and high registers are more difficult. The easiest register is generally the middle. If there are harmonics or overtones present when playing in the low register, the second and third registers are easier and can be played with more confidence.

Most inexperienced players will benefit from a few minutes daily practice on harmonics to establish air speed and a richer tone. Play low C and then overblow it until the octave sounds; then blow harder to get the third harmonic, and carry on through the whole series of harmonics as far as you can. The upper ones can be unstable or difficult, depending on the player and the flute.

Learn exactly where to place the notes without them 'cracking' or 'splitting'.

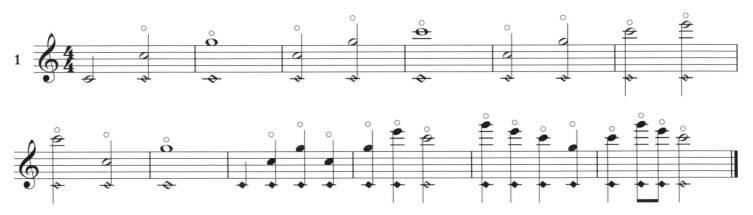

Try some bugle calls to learn how to pass from one harmonic to the other with confidence.

Repeat the three exercises using the fingering for low C♯, D and E♭.
Notice the increase of air speed required for the higher harmonics.

THE LOW REGISTER

This is the most sensible place to begin tone exercises, the low register being the fundamental tone of the flute and the foundation upon which the upper notes depend. Your teacher may advise you to start elsewhere but you can return to these exercises later.

Make a choice, perhaps guided by your teacher: either start on the exercises below, or turn to p.10, the 'Tone Colour Exercises'. It all depends on your level: if you are a relative beginner, start on the B below. A more advanced player may be better practising tone colour exercises.

To start, practise a B. This is an easy note to play because the flute tube is almost at its shortest length and the finger and thumb are holding the flute securely, whereas the two notes above B may be less secure. Play this B for as long as it takes to obtain a clear, bright, rich and beautiful note, perhaps the best B you have ever played. It may take five minutes or more to do this, but the effort will be worth it. You will achieve more for your tone by practising a beautiful B than you would by playing pages of exercises.

Don't play a series of short notes; play each B for as long as your breath lasts. When the B is really the best you can play, begin Exercise 1. Each pair of notes should use up all of your breath, so play it as slowly as you can. Try to play each pair with the same tone quality and match them up one with the other, as you descend. Take care not to turn the flute in on your lip when descending, or to lower your head; this might appear to make the note more resonant, but will also flatten the pitch. If the second note sounds better than the first, play the pair of notes in reverse.

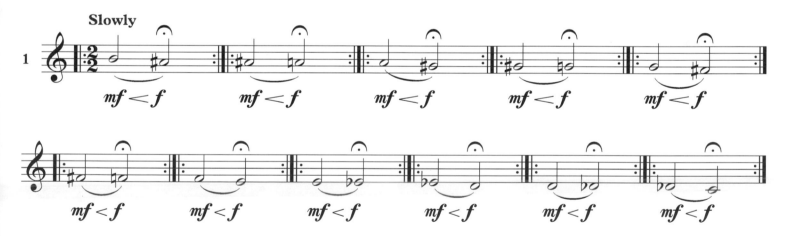

Don't force the tone in the final bars. It is may be more difficult to get a good tone here and you may need to repeat these last few bars several times.

During the first few days, Exercise 1 may take fifteen minutes or more. This is fine and there are no prizes for the fastest performance. After a few days of practice, a common complaint is that your tone appears to be worse! This is normal because having spent a lot of time listening to long notes, your perception of your tone is more sensitive. Probably your tone has improved, but while playing notes for long periods critically, you can hear what is wrong. You may be more aware of your tonal deficiencies, which is constructive and will lead to a better tone.

After a week or more, in stages, add Exercises 2, 3 and 4 to your practice. Repeat each bar as often as necessary, not because it is printed in that way, but because you need it!

It is all a question of *time, patience* and *intelligent work*.

Start your practice time with the reference tone, a bright B natural.

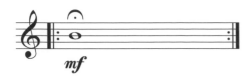

* These last few notes become progressively more difficult and this is because the tube length is longer and offers more resistance the lower you descend. Notice that you *crescendo* as you descend. This will help strengthen the lower notes.

You can now add these next exercises to your repertoire of long tones. Make the small adjustments to your lips as you descend so that each note is the best that you can play. Take care not to turn the lip plate in, or to lower your head when descending as the tone can sound buzzy – like a bag full of wasps! Keep your tone warm, and remember to practise the B first.

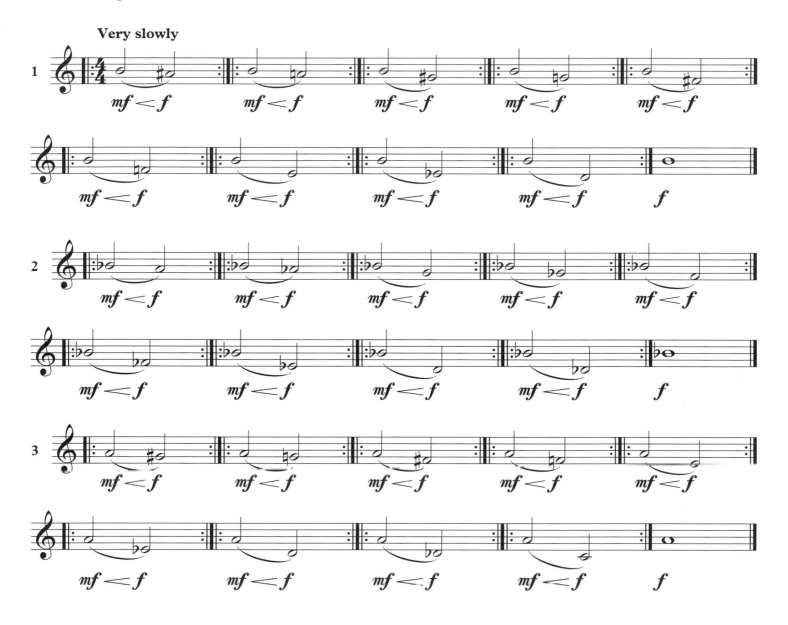

As you become more advanced, you may like to change to a different way of thinking about tone. Instead of just 'a beautiful tone', you should examine the different colours obtainable on the flute. There is no doubt that the flute can produce a relatively wide variety of colours, all dependent on the player.

INTONATION AND TONE COLOUR

These exercises are designed to encourage you to play with a variety of tone colours, especially in the low register. You will also need to make use of a wide variety of nuances, playing louder and softer, as these are a part of an expressive tone and of the expression of music. If you are relatively new to these exercises, it would be best to check on your pitch control before going further as this will save you time in the long term.

Start with the pitch bending exercise on p.39. This is the foundation upon which you will build up your knowledge both of playing loudly and softly and of *crescendo* and *diminuendo*, while remaining perfectly in tune.

If you are already familiar with this technique then you may go on to the next section on Tone Colour.

TONE COLOUR EXERCISES Three Colours

This section contains tone exercises with a different objective, that of obtaining a variety of tone colours. This will make music making more interesting both for the audience and the player. The colours most commonly used are described as 'dark' and rich, and 'light' or hollow. For simplicity, we will use 'purple' and 'yellow' to describe these two extremes of colour. Then you will practise an in-between colour for 'everyday' use.

If you need a more detailed explanation on how to obtain these colours, it can be found in *Proper Flute Playing* (Novello), and in *Practice Book 6 - Advanced Practice* and *Efficient Practice* (Falls House Press). There are three low register exercises to work on:

1) The 'Aquarium' variation from *Carnival of the Animals* by Saint-Saens to practise a pure, hollow or yellow tone.

2) A theme from Ravel's *Introduction and Allegro* for septet. This is to practise a dark, purple, rich tone.

3) An exercise based on Debussy's *Prelude à l'après-midi d'un faune*. This is for practice after working on the first two colours and is to help obtain a 'midway tone' – neither dark nor light.

1) Begin with the Aquarium, the first exercise in D minor, then tackle the keys above and below it. In the first example the task is to make the low D the same colour as the previous A. When moving a 5th downwards, it is hard to keep to the same colour. If so, practise only the second half of the exercise from the point marked ★. The step-by-step method will help you play from A down to D without changing the colour.

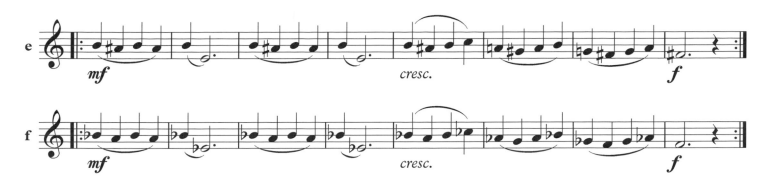

2) The Ravel Theme: the best method to get a dark colour – without making the tone flat and small – is first to practise the 'Aquarium' tune with a 'yellow' colour, then – without turning the headjoint inwards or lowering your head, use your lips and jaw to blow down into the mouth hole to get a darker colour. Remember to do this without turning the flute in. Just keep the same mouth position but blow in a more downwards direction without covering. It might sound rather rough at first, but it will soon clear when you get accustomed to it. Don't play this tune too slowly as it should ideally be played in one breath. Note the *crescendo* when descending.

THEME

3) The Debussy Theme: try out your two colours (dark and light) in this tune and then take the middle road between the two, which will be your 'everyday' tone. Start with small steps of just three notes as shown in (a). Always *crescenado* downwards as it is what the flute is not good at doing. Practise what the flute can't do well. Go on to practise (b) after a few days and finally, when your breath and tone allow it, go on to (c) and (d).

FINAL EXERCISE

THE MIDDLE REGISTER I

When the lower register has been practised with some interesting new colours, these need to be spread into the second octave. You will notice that however easy it was to get two different colours in the low register, it is more difficult in the second octave. But you don't want to have two colours in the low register and only one in the middle octave. Making a 'yellow' tone in the second octave is much easier than getting the darker, 'purple' colour, but the exercises below will make it easier to hear and to achieve the desired result.

Remember one important point: as you rise to middle E, avoid raising the airstream or air direction. We all have a tendency to do this without realising it because it helps to get middle E more cleanly and smoothly. E is a note which tends to crack or 'split' if blown too hard. However, with some intelligent and patient work, a lot can be gained with a little expenditure of time.

You will start by practising the first 4 bars of the first exercise with a yellow colour and before beginning, go back to refresh your memory with the 'Aquarium' melody in 'yellow' (on p.10). Then begin the exercise, trying to keep the 'yellow' colour up to middle E. After a few days at this, with the same exercise, move on to the darker 'purple' colour but this time keep the air direction low, avoiding raising it to make middle E easier. In this colour, the E will often break up and crack. This is quite alright as you are discovering just how this happens; then you can practise getting middle E without cracking it (also see *Proper Flute Playing*).

* Use a dark colour to help the leap into the upper note.

THE MIDDLE REGISTER II

Instead of approaching the middle octave from the low register as in the previous exercise, we can also try spreading the two colours upwards simply by playing slurred octaves but again, without raising the airstream to do so. The principals of practising are the same as in the previous exercise.

First, work at these 5 notes with your best 'yellow' tone. Then begin, slurring the first octave without too much tension. The upper note will sound thin if you raise the airstream. Pitch is important here too: if the upper B is sharper than the lower B, then keep the airstream low when ascending.

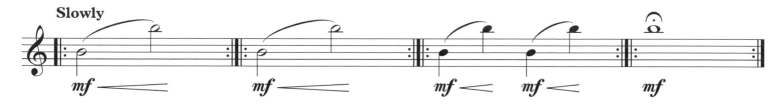

When the upper B is beautiful, begin Exercise 1 spreading this tone down to the lower notes step-by-step. Be sure the B really is beautiful before making the A♯ just as good. As in earlier exercises, play each pair of notes for your full breath's worth. Only proceed downwards if the previous pair of notes are the best you can achieve. Perhaps the second note sounds better than the first note? If that happens, reverse the exercise to make the first as good as the second note.

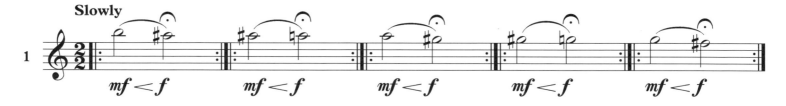

As you continue down, it should all go fairly well as far as G, but from here down to the left hand C in the lower register, there are some problems to overcome. The area from F♯ to E inclusive can easily crack or break up if blown too hard. Then the E♭ and D have a slightly different colour to the notes around them. From D to C♯ there is always a change of colour. These differences must be ironed out and in these exercises you can find out just how far you can push these notes before they break up. Evenness of tone is what you are striving for. As before, when the lower note of each pair is better, to match them up, reverse the exercise to improve the upper one.

When some improvement has been made, go back to B natural.

Be sure that the first finger is always raised* for E♭ and D. Raising the first finger clears them of tonal stuffiness. If these notes still present a problem, try the sequential steps below to help correct it.

After some days of practice, add Exercise 4 to your daily practice. It joins two bars of Exercise 1 together. The tone quality should be the same.

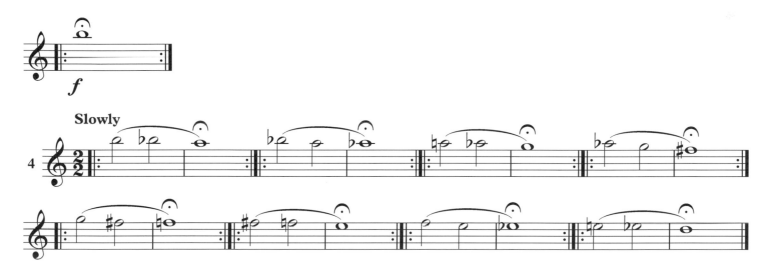

When these differences of tone have been largely ironed out, add Exercises 5 and 6 to your repertoire:

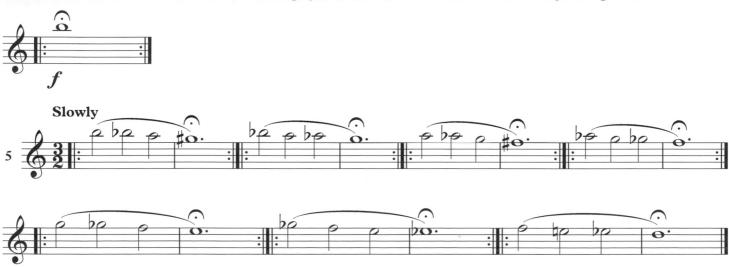

* Exercises for this problem can be found in *Practice Book 2 – Technique* and *Practice Book 3 – Articulation*.

Slowly

6

The last bar of Exercise 6 will remind you of the difficulty we all have with the difference both in tone and colour with C♯ which is also dealt with in the next section, 'Problem Notes'. As you descend, the C♯ seems isolated and empty. The reason for the most part, is that the C♯ hole is smaller because it is used jointly by other notes, a multi-purpose hole – and the reason why it is small. (It is 7mm or less in diameter).

First practise the lowest C♯, and then overblow it to the next octave higher, the upper C♯; do this without moving any fingers. This second harmonic C♯ is rich and full of overtones. Now slur on to the correct fingering – the open C♯ – trying to maintain the same colour and – just as important – the same pitch.

C♯ on many flutes sounds a little more resonant if you add the second and third fingers of the right hand to the usual fingering, with all fingers off. It helps to stabilise it.* Notice that the upper C natural sounds more resonant than C♯ because it has a larger tone hole of around 13mm.

7

Again, carefully compare the tuning of the left-hand C and C♯ with the second harmonics of the low C and C♯. Additional help and exercises can be found on pages 42-43 in this book. It is a waste of time playing a C or C♯ with a good tone if the intonation is defective.

Now work at C and C♯ sharp from the lower register.

Slowly

8

sonore

* The upper C♯, known as C♯2 has long been a problem note for the flute. Since 2012, some flute makers have adopted a new scale, known as RS 2012, which should make C♯2 easier to manage.

If this last exercise has helped you, then try smoothing out the differences between all the notes from C♯ to E, approaching them from the lower register.

Then from B, work back up again, attempting to smooth out any differences. Play each two bars in one breath.

Finally, in Exercise 11 you will try to play with an even tone of whatever colour from upper B down to low C or B. Start off with pairs of notes as in Exercise 1, and as you progress, add more notes to the sequence – using Exercises 4, 5 and 6 as your pattern until you can play the 7-note exercise below.

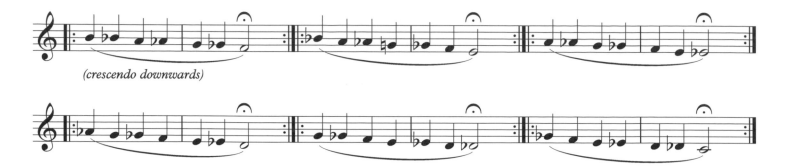

(crescendo downwards)

You should now be a long way towards solving the tone and colour problems of the middle register. Perhaps your tone will not be entirely even throughout these two octaves but you will have learnt enough information and gained the tools to enable you to tackle any problem areas.

It's all a matter of .... , ... and .... !

THE HIGH REGISTER

The higher notes are more difficult both to colour and to obtain depth of tone with good sonority. The work you have already done on the first two octaves will greatly help in tackling the third octave. You would be wise to read the section which follows: **Problem Notes** Third Octave Intonation (p.25).

If necessary, the techniques discussed there can be incorporated into the exercises which follow. It is better for your lips not to practise the third octave just after practising the first two octaves. Perhaps the best time would be at the end of your practice session when you have had time to recover and relax.

The aim here is to iron out differences of colour between the middle and top registers and at the same time to enhance the tone quality. Trying to get different colours is quite difficult in the third octave but it can be done. Remember the earlier advice? Don't raise the airstream too much as you play into the third octave. This is easier said than done, perhaps because the top notes are easier when the air is directed upwards – but the tone will be thinner and you should avoid this. More importantly, the third octave generally suffers from being too sharp. This is mostly a built-in acoustical problem which can be corrected with intelligent practice by the use of the airstream. Small differences can be made between 'yellow' and 'purple' tones but only when the airstream is kept lower to avoid becoming too sharp. Check with a tuner in both *forte, piano* as well as in *crescendo* and *diminuendo* in the 3rd octave.

It's just a question of *time, patience* and *intelligent work* – plus understanding neighbours!

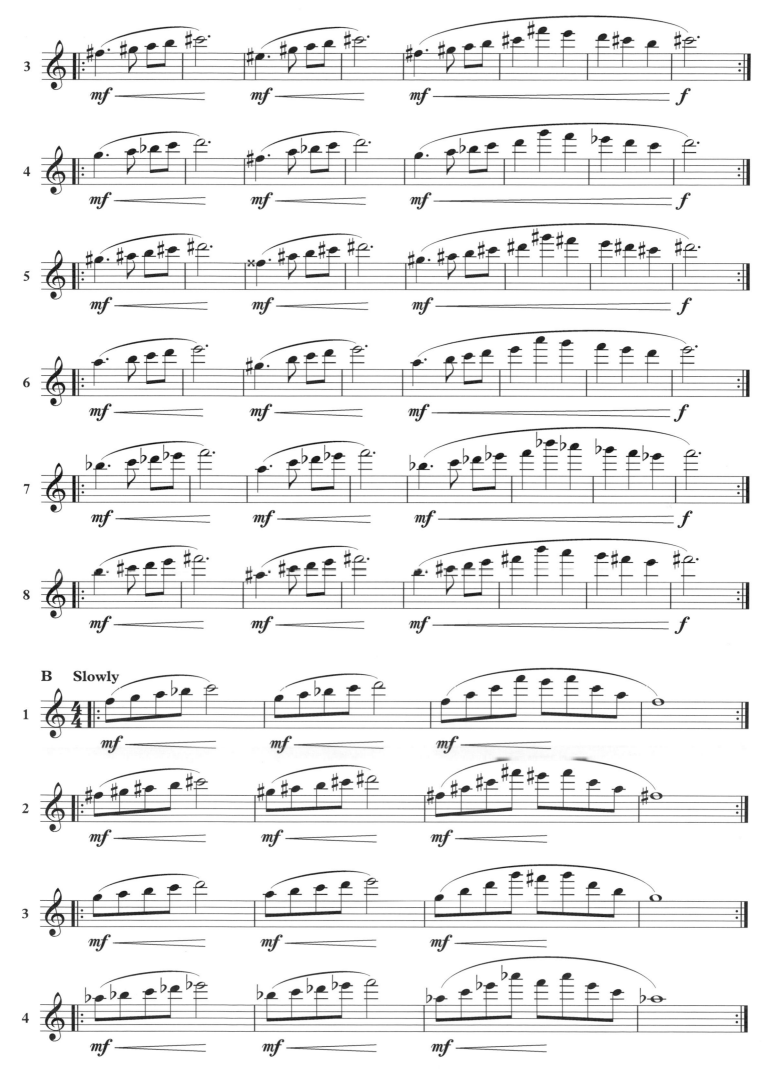

The following exercises are either an alternative or an additional form of 3rd octave exercise. Try to avoid tension as you ascend. If you wish to include some 4th octave notes then do so only when your embouchure is sufficiently strong.

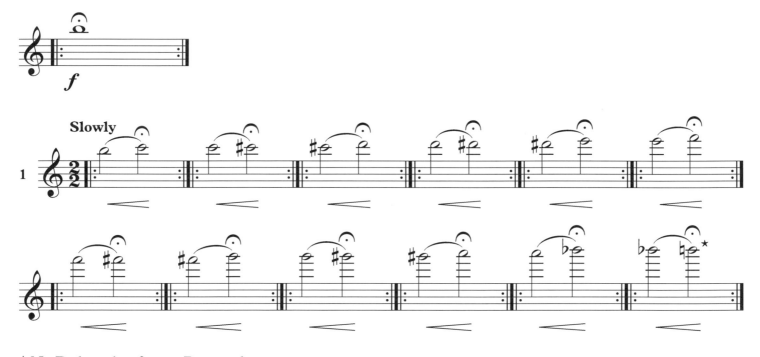

* No D sharp key for top B natural

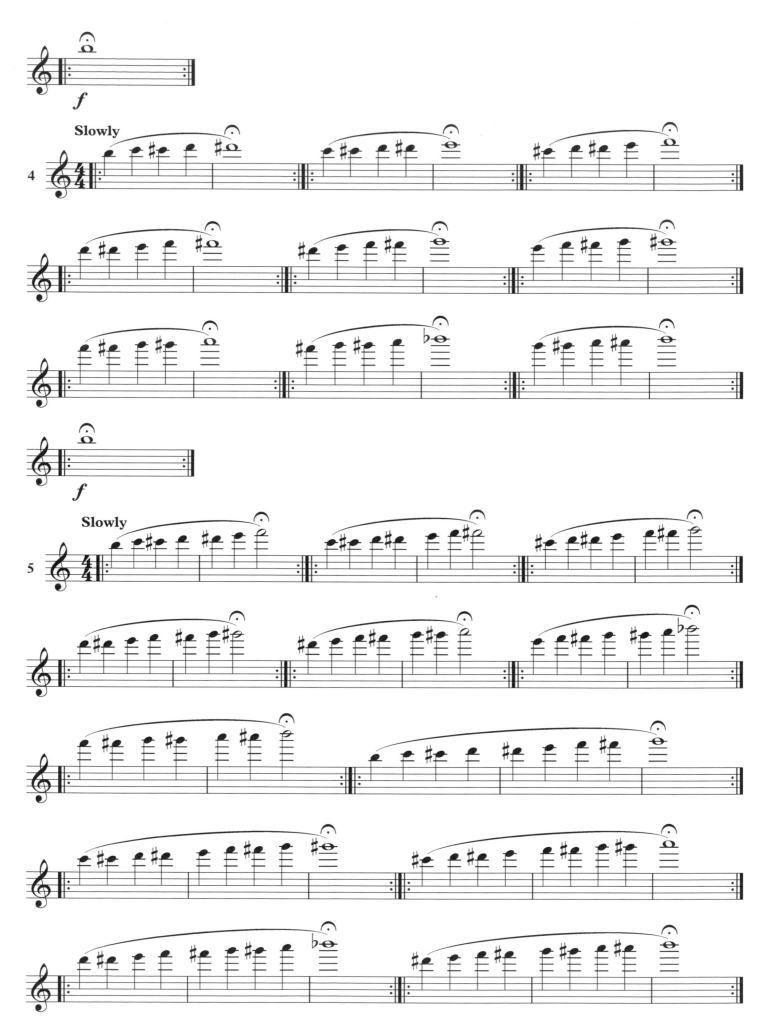

As your lips become more developed you will need to change the nuances and add *crescendos* and *diminuendos* so as to make the exercises more musical and challenging.

PROBLEM NOTES Third Octave Intonation

You may have noticed that the top E and F♯ are sharp in pitch. It is important to know that almost every note of the 3rd octave has an intonation problem, most of them suffering from being sharp. To answer your unasked question: they can't be fixed without interfering with the tuning of the first two octaves! What we have to do is use all the tools you have practised so far to make these notes better in tune. The first point is: have you correctly studied the Pitch Control exercises on p. 39? If not, that is where you will have to start. What follows from there on will rely on your possessing these tools and using them effectively.

The worst notes for being prone to sharpness are top E and F♯. There is a mechanical solution for this problem in a 'split E' mechanism, though this only partly repairs the E. If this mechanism is used, logically a 'split F♯' mechanism should also be fitted, but this is a much more costly addition to the flute and complicated too. For that reason, split F♯s are rarely seen.

Both E and F♯ are a little more difficult to emit than their surrounding notes and there is a mechanical reason why this is so. In the low register, play from low E♭ up to B♭ with the usual fingering. Now finger – without blowing – the same notes in the 3rd octave. In each case there is usually one finger or key difference between the 1st and 3rd octaves. That is, except for E and F♯ which have two holes open, and large ones too. This reduces the resistance and makes them harder to play with stability and also makes them sharp as well, though the difference in difficulty between, say E and F, is small but enough to cause problems. For both these notes, the two extra holes which open can be closed if a 'split E' or 'split F♯' mechanism is fitted. Another solution (an easier one) is to take off your little finger – the 'pinky' – for top E. This will flatten it sufficiently.

If those were the only problem notes in the 3rd octave, then probably all flutes would have them. But there are other notes which also have difficulties: G♯, B and C. You may need to look at alternative fingerings for those. The two common problem notes, E and F♯, can with practice, be mastered, making the extra mechanism unnecessary. To learn how, play the scale of G. Notice that you need to increase the air speed as you ascend, using more for E and F♯ than for the other notes. This makes these two notes louder.

The solution is to play *all the notes* in the scale with a faster air speed than necessary. Not only will this help your tone, but it will also remove the problem. To make these two notes even more secure, use your faster air speed *as you approach the problem note*. In other words, the problem isn't with E and F♯: it is with the notes just before them which need extra air speed. Think carefully about this before practising these exercises below.

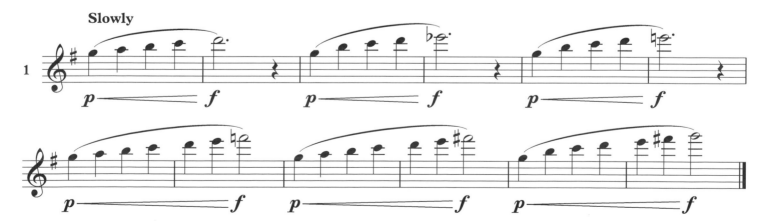

As E natural and F♯ are rather sharp notes, compare their pitch with the harmonic E and F♯ as shown below.

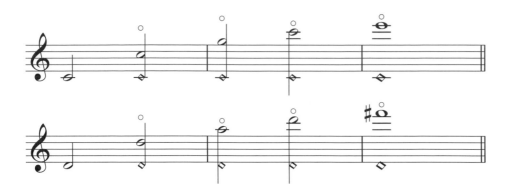

The other problem notes are D above the stave, E♭ and G♯. These notes are variable on any individual flute as the makers are not always in agreement about the placing of the tone holes, or the 'scale' of the flute.* The 3rd octave D is usually flat and E♭ and G♯ are very sharp notes. These notes can be controlled with the lips, especially D as there are no easy fingering solutions to help you out of trouble here! E♭ can be carefully lipped down when sharp, while for top G♯, a less easily moveable note, you can use the alternative 'long fingering' found in *Practice Book 6*. Work at these exercises, taking the greatest care about the intonation so that you 'program' your lips and jaw to deal with them.

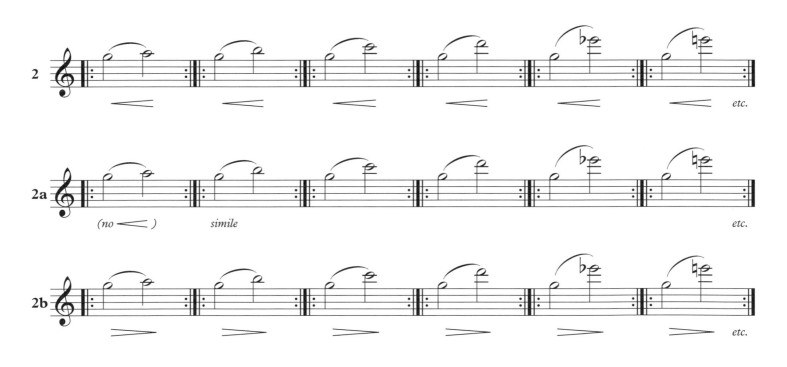

If those were difficult, you can try these exercises as a way around the problem:

* See footnote on p.18

Repeat the previous exercise but with a *diminuendo*:

Finally, repeat the first exercise but with a *diminuendo*:

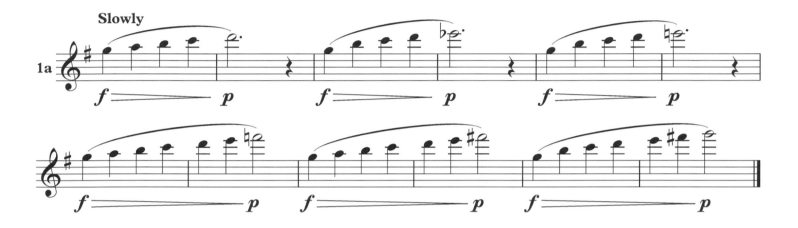

You can now go back to the earlier exercises for the High Register, starting on p.20, bearing all these points in mind as you practise.

ADVANCED TONE COLOUR

You have already practised the Tone Colour exercises on pages 10-14, using different melodies to help acquire yellow and purple tones. The flute is capable of producing a great variety of tone colours and you should use your new skill by transferring it into arpeggio exercises and then into pieces.

Play the first exercise with a strong, dark, purple colour; use this for major keys. Then change colour for the minor keys. Use a full purple tone for the major keys and a quieter, softer, yellow tone for the minor ones.

Tone Colour Exercise I

When changing from major to minor, make the biggest difference in tone colour that you can between the two colours. In the middle octave, a darker colour is much more difficult and we have a tendency to use the less focused hollow colour in the middle register for both exercises! Keep practising to push the two colours apart.

Play these from memory if you can and play through as many keys each day as possible. The full exercise can be found in *The Complete Daily Exercises* (Novello). There are many other major/minor exercises like the one below in that book.

Continue in the following key sequence: E♭ major; C minor; A♭ Major, F minor and so on, through the 24 keys. You may find that each key suggests its own colour. After some weeks of practice, add Exercise II to your repertoire. The full sequence of keys can be found in *The Complete Daily Exercises* (Novello).

Tone Colour Exercise II

Remember to make a big tone colour change when moving on to exercise B.

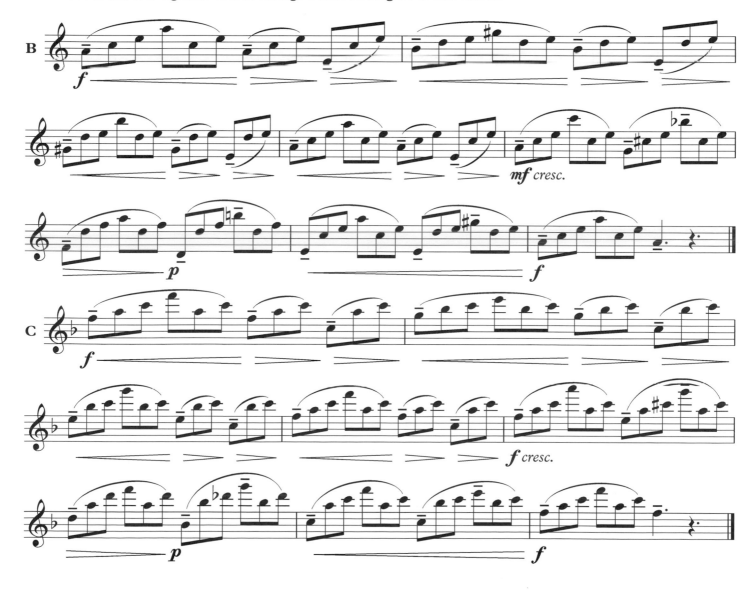

If you wish, continue the sequence in E♭, C minor, A♭ and so on. The complete exercise, with many others, can be found in *The Complete Daily Exercises* (Novello). Finally choose some melodies with which you can practise your tone colours. Some are found at the back of this book. Others can be found in *Flute Solos*, Volumes 1, 2 and 3 (Novello) and in *A Rameau Album*; *A Couperin Album* and *A Vivaldi Album* (Novello).

BREATH CONTROL

A good teacher is invaluable in setting you right about a good breathing technique. A full explanation can also be found in *Practice Book 5 – Breathing and Scales*. The techniques outlined below are in addition to these and will be useful in controlling the air stream and for gaining skill in playing for a long time without a breath.

Whistle Tones

These are useful for controlling the flow of the air stream and controlling the abdominal muscles which drive the air from your body. Whistle tones are the almost inaudible little squeaks which often sound accidentally at the end or at the beginning of a quiet note. We usually practise to avoid them! They are played lightly and with relaxed lips. Play G in the low register, blowing softly and lightly. Making an 'oo' shape with your lips and rolling out may help. When you find one, hold on to it as long as you can. In the beginning, they come and go, but the exercise is in holding the same whistle tone steadily. Low C also produces a lot of easy whistle tones and hardly any air is needed for these notes. A few minutes each day will be useful practice.

Length

Play a middle B for as long as possible and check your timing with a clock or timer. If you have read the breathing section on *Practice Book 5*, then simply do the exercises, and redo this test each week and compare the results. Even those with a small body size can get extraordinary results after a few months. Take care to play the B in tune; don't roll in to make it easier – it's cheating!

FLEXIBILTY

To play a single note with a good tone is not difficult. It needs the right combination of air speed, direction, and lip position in relation to the embouchure hole. When we move to another note, these ingredients have to alter slightly to play this note with an equally good tone. In fact, each note has its own air speed, air direction and lip position. In some parts of the flute compass, these changes are very small; in others, such as in the region of the left hand C♯s, you may have to make bigger changes to get a good tone on each note. Moving from one note to another requires instant but smooth changes to these ingredients. This is what these next exercises are about. The bigger the interval, the more difficult it is to move smoothly from one note to another. With the right practice, and _____, _____ and _____ _____, you will soon make big intervals with ease.

Think about these points when practising these next exercises:

Intonation is paramount; check again with the Pitch Control exercise on p. 39 in this book. The flute has a natural tendency to play louder as it goes up. Most instruments do the opposite. You too should do the opposite; play louder as you go down and softer – but in tune – when ascending. Think about the intervals: moving from E♭ to B♭ is easy to play smoothly, but when moving on to the upper G, is there a bump between the notes? Can you play from B♭ to G really smoothly? Can you do it without playing the G louder – in fact, can you play the G softer? If not, use the exercises at the end to help you. Consider these flexibility exercises as part of your daily practice. There are several other technical exercises like this in *Complete Daily Exercises* which can be played slowly for flexibility.

Flexibility I

Slowly and freely ♩ = 60-88

after Sousseman

These extra exercises will help get the lips functioning well:

Next, practise in this way, gradually working up to the upper G so that it can be played softly but *in tune*. Make these intervals without undue strain or tension.

Then practise the whole exercise in these different ways:

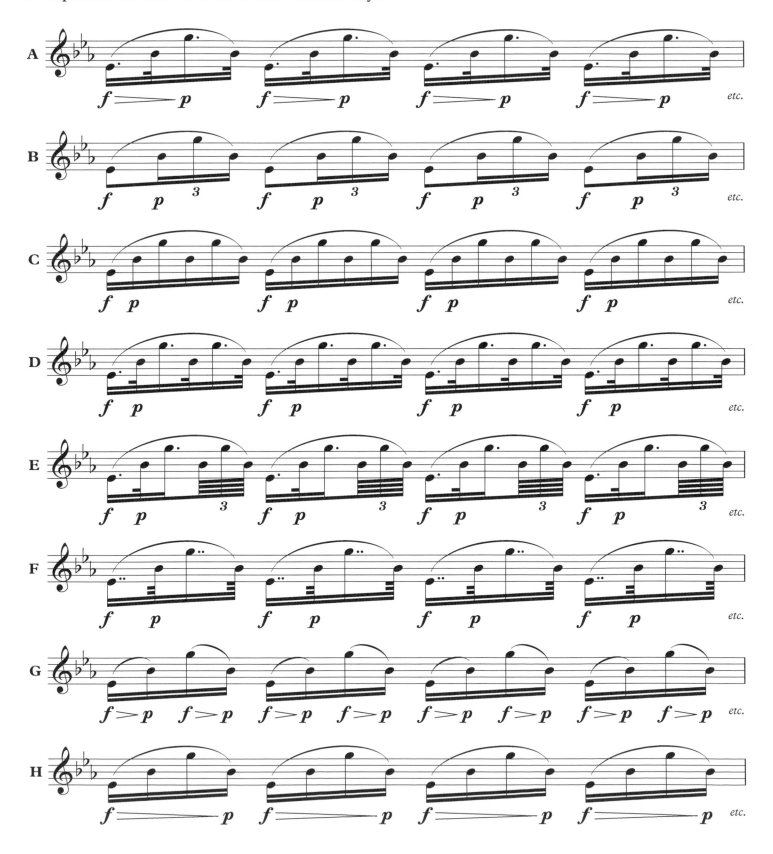

Carefully follow the nuances: ask yourself, 'Am I playing really softly and really loudly?
The 'Tone Colour – Exercise II' on p.29 can also be practised in this way.

Flexibility II (Andersen, Op. 63, No.12)

This is a much more difficult exercise and should be attempted only by the advanced player.

As before, there are ways to practise this to get a good result, as shown:

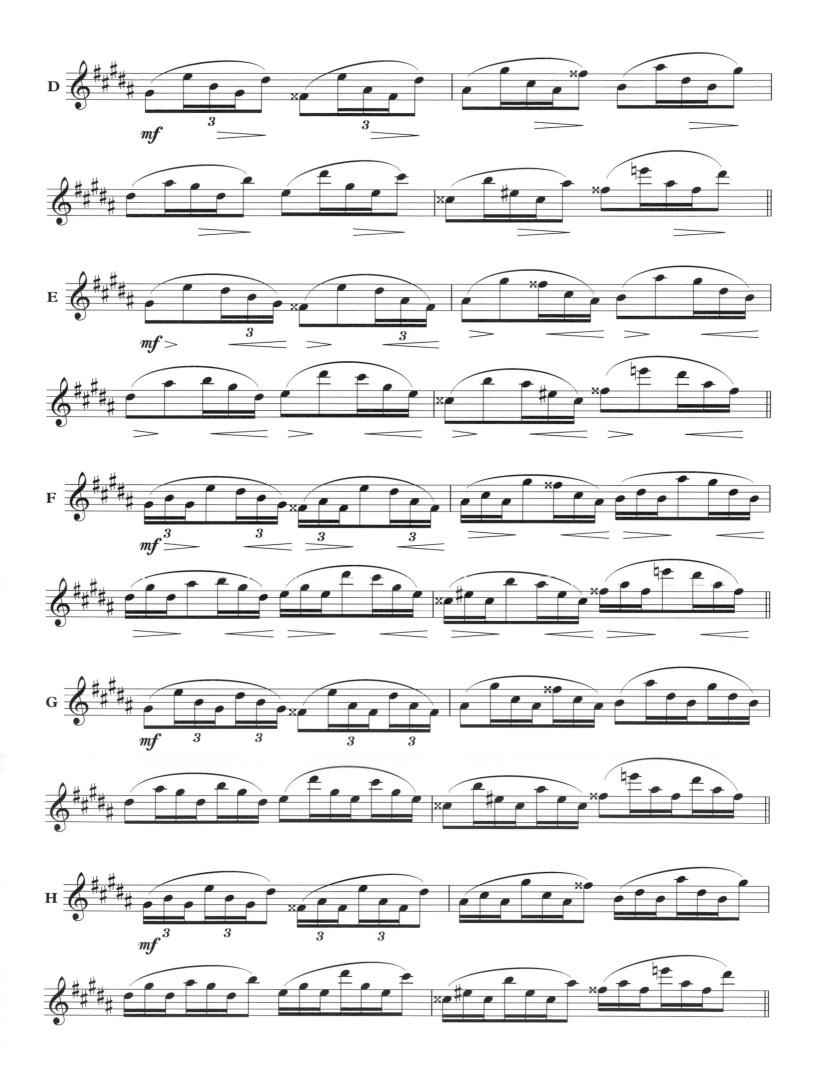

Many studies and daily exercises will be useful to you if practised in this way. Some can be found in *The Complete Daily Exercises* (Novello). Some examples illustrating flexibility in the common flute repertoire can also be found at the end of this book.

PROBLEMS BOX

1. The exercises are tiring? They certainly are! Be sure to warm up your lips before tackling them. An athlete would spend some time doing warm-up exercises before a race or training.

2. Difficulties with intonation? See the 'Pitch Control' section on the next page.

3. Moving your lips/jaw a lot to get the next note? Don't worry too much about this. Getting the right result is the first goal. Afterwards, you can concentrate on getting the same good result but at the same time reducing the movement.

PITCH CONTROL

Playing in tune is inseparable from a beautiful musical performance. To play expressively, the performer is required to play loudly, softly and all the different levels in between, and in addition, make *crescendos* and *diminuendos* too. The superior player will also use tone colours to enhance their music making. All these attributes need careful control of the lips and jaw and of the air direction. This is accomplished in step-by-step exercises to gain the necessary tools and assist the ears to understand how to practise well. This section covers ways to acquire these valuable tools and so make music beautiful.

Play a left hand C, fortissimo, and make a total diminuendo without making any movement of the jaw or lips, until the note disappears. The note will most likely go flat.

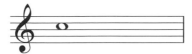

To prevent it becoming flat you need to acquire a few tools and practise some simple steps. Play the C natural, but this time, bend the note downwards by moving only your jaw and lips. This will change the air direction and cover the hole a little. Using only your jaw and lips, try to flatten the C until it becomes a B♭ or even an A. If this movement is not enough to get a B♭, then use your head as well. Don't move your arms or hands. If you don't succeed straight away, try it a few times more. Most players can get a B♭ and some even an A.

Now play the same C again, only this time bend it upwards. You might be lucky to get a C♯/D♭ but most people will only succeed in making the C somewhat sharper. This note-bending exercise is good for making the lips and jaw more flexible, and is valuable for finding a good lip position and the right tone colour at the beginning of a practice session. Spend a few days practising the note-bending exercise until you can get an A.

This next jazzy exercise is for fun but is also useful for establishing a flexible embouchure, which will pay dividends in your future practice and performances.

This exercise uses the note-bending you have just practised but you will need to move faster between the second and third notes and with more accuracy. First, play through the first 4 bars, fingering the third note normally. Then repeat it but finger the third note with the same fingering as the second note. Bend it down with your jaw and lips, and if necessary with your head too. If you need to, use a reduced air speed as well to get the flatter note. It is not easy to get the rhythm and the pitch right at the same time!

NOTE ENDINGS and Nuances

If you spend time on these two exercises, it becomes clear that, in a *diminuendo*, as the air speed is reduced and the pitch goes flat, so the embouchure hole (the blow hole) needs to be uncovered to compensate for this drop in pitch. This action will make the note sharper, returning it back to its correct pitch. The simultaneous movements of air speed, jaw, lips and perhaps the head too, have to be co-ordinated and practised together before achieving any long-term result.

In the next exercise, the tone is gradually and smoothly made softer without the note becoming flat. Play each note for 4 beats so that *regulation* is introduced into the exercise – that of controlling loud and soft playing according to a set time. Your head should be down and your jaw back for the forte, gradually raising the airstream, uncovering the mouth hole and keeping the pitch exactly the same during the *diminuendo*. Make sure that you keep your arms still; *don't turn the flute in with your hands* as you practise this exercise.

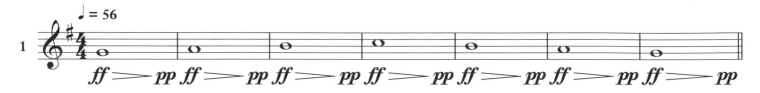

After a few days, move on to Exercise 2. You may notice that as you move towards middle D, the notes are easier to control. This is because the tube is shorter: the further up you go, the easier it is to control the pitch. When D is reached, and the notes above, controlling the pitch is a little more difficult and may require more movement. Middle E is a difficult note too, due to the length of the tube at that point, but on continuing up the scale, there will be fewer difficulties.

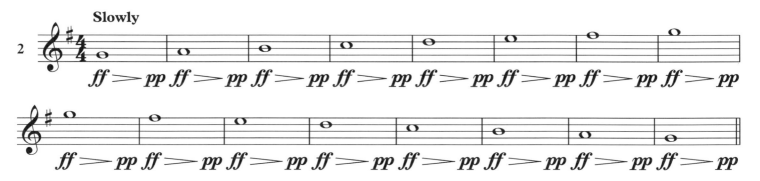

After a few days, go on to Exercises 3–6, though don't be too impatient to move on. Each exercise shortens the time taken to keep the tone at the correct pitch and you should be in perfect control of each exercise before moving on to the harder ones. Use your tuner to check the pitch. You will see by now that this is how pitch is controlled and how tone colours are handled and how players play expressively. It is perhaps the most vital part of your flute study. The long term aim is *musical communication*.

After practising the 'Short Endings' (Exercise 6) you can see that these can be added to a note of any length or loudness; you can end the note quickly without it dropping in pitch. As you become more proficient in this technique and use your jaw/lips and the airspeed more thoughtfully and effectively, so your head movement is likely to decrease. These will be the essential tools to use in being expressive.

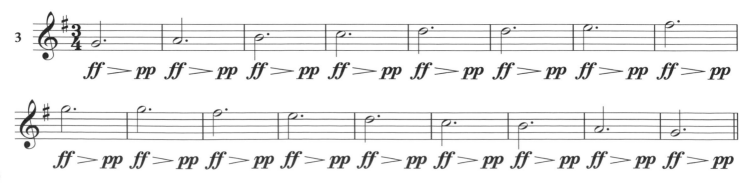

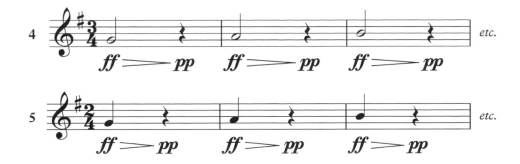

SHORT ENDINGS

Finally, test yourself on this next exercise: can you remain at the same pitch when *forte* and *piano*?

T.W.

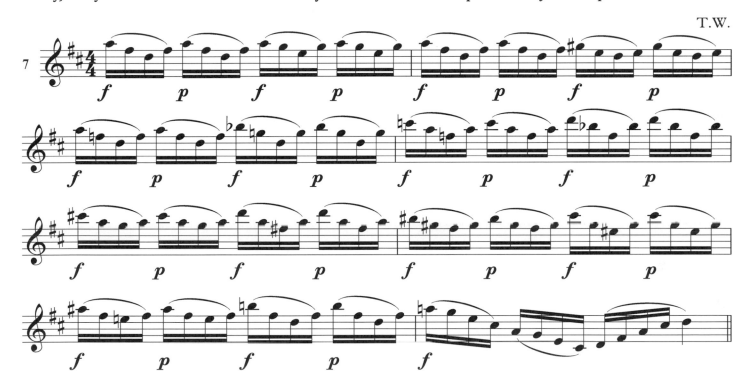

This is a final expressive study to check all the tools you have gained so far. Go back to earlier exercises if there are problems in pitch with this little study. Check it with a tuning device.

T.W.

INTONATION OF C♯ and the Trill Key Notes

C♯ is often an unstable note.* More about this problem will be found in *Practice Book Four – Intonation & Vibrato*. Below are some simple checks to help control this note and the C in the left hand, as well as the trill key notes – D and D♯ – during trills.

First, check the pitch of your C natural – the left hand one – with the pitch of your low C with all fingers on. Play the low C first, and without taking the right hand little finger off the low keys, overblow on to the C an octave above to compare the pitch. They should be the same. If the upper C is sharp, you should pull the headjoint out a little until the two Cs are identical.

Repeat this for C♯, first the low one and then the 'open' one. This left hand C♯ is more difficult to control and make steady. *Practice Book 4* will suggest mechanical solutions if it is too sharp compared to the C, but here we are concerned just with its quality.

You can practise these next two exercises to check the quality and pitch of the C and C♯ notes. The second exercise compares the C with the 3rd harmonic of F – which is also C.

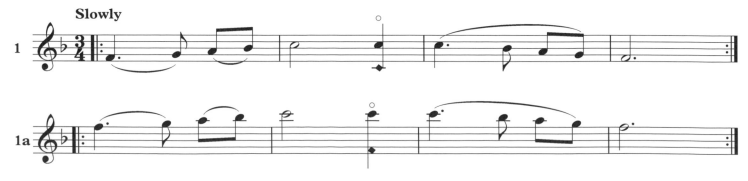

* See also p.18

Now do the same with these two exercises for checking C♯.

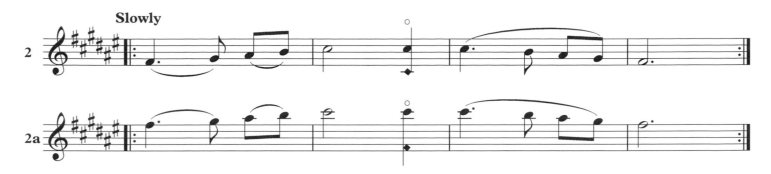

Next is a much quicker comparison between the harmonic note and the natural note. They must sound at the same pitch.

T.W.

Play the previous exercises before attempting to check the tuning of your trill keys with the exercises below. The trill key notes are in effect the notes D and D♯, using small multi-use tone holes. These tone holes are about the same size as the small C♯ tone hole. In Exercise 4, finger C but add the first trill key which will then sound D. In the second exercise, No. 5, finger C with the first trill which will produce D – as before, but in the second bar, finger C, adding the second trill key. That will produce E♭. Play them both with as good a tone as you can get, as if using the normal fingering. Note the fingering:

1 – Finger C but add the first trill key
2 – Finger C but add the second trill key

In exercise 6, use these trill fingerings alternating with the usual ones. It makes a good comparison study.

In this study No. 7, you can pretend that, at a concert, your foot joint fell off! But you have to carry on playing using the trill key fingerings and almost without using the foot-joint – except for one note, the low D which you can play an octave above if you wish.

In the next two exercises, use the normal fingerings but check the tuning of C in No. 8 and C# in No. 9.

For further study of intonation and for studies to practise, use the 24 Studies in *Practice Book 4*. There is one in every key and they are specially written to help you become more sensitive to 'just' intonation where notes are bent so as to play better in tune.

EXAMPLES: Melodies from the Flute Repertoire

TONE COLOUR

In these musical extracts, the imaginative flute player can endeavour to capture the spirit of the piece through the use of tone colour.

SICILIENNE

MADRIGAL

The tone colours can be chosen to match up to the harmony through which the melody passes.

PAVANE

PRELUDE À L'APRÈS-MIDI D'UN FAUNE

This is a good test of breath control. It is common, though not obligatory, to play this solo in one breath, although some conductors ask for one or even two extra breaths to be taken.

DANSE MACABRE

SINFONIA FROM CANTATA NO. 156

FLEXIBILITY

These are some examples of how a player needs flexibility to play well. See also *Complete Daily Exercises* where there is a study based on this piece.

PERPETUUM MOBILE

Piccolo

J. STRAUSS

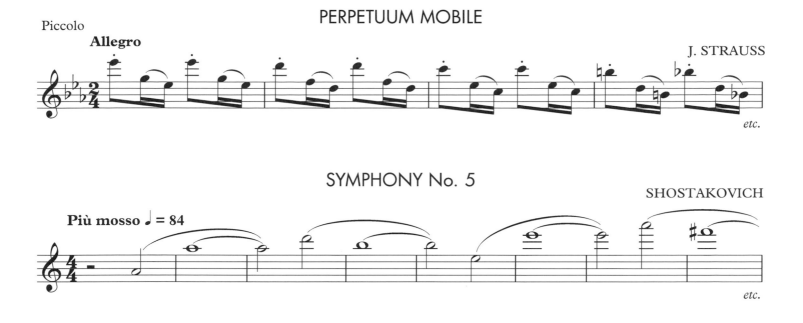

SYMPHONY No. 5

SHOSTAKOVICH

OVERTURE: WILLIAM TELL

ROSSINI

VARIATIONS ON A THEME OF HAYDN

VARIATION VII

BRAHMS

FINALE

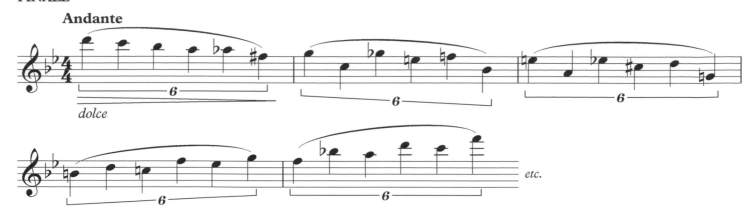

SONATE EN CONCERT

SICILIENNE

J-M. DAMASE[1]

PITCH CONTROL

The flute repertoire abounds with examples of music which contain difficult quiet passages, or *diminuendo* problems. Though all the following are solo works, the pitch must remain correct.

SYRINX

DEBUSSY

PIÈCE

IBERT[2]

DANSE DE LA CHÈVRE

HONEGGER[3]